TEXT FAILS

THE COMICAL WORLD OF AUTOCORRECT
FAILS, SUPER FUNNY TEXT MESSAGES
FAILS, HILARIOUS AND CRAZY
SMARTPHONE MISHAPS.

By Ryan Brown

INTRODUCTION

At some point in our lives, we have sent or received junk texts from friends, colleagues, or even our family members. Some of these texts are very embarrassing.

Since the inception and integration of some basic forms of Artificial Intelligence (AI) into smartphones, auto-correcting sentences and words has become inevitable.

So, extra caution has to be taken before sending messages! This book is a collection of funny and hilarious text fails. Read and Enjoy!

1) Going to bed..

Jackson: Hi Babe! What are you doing?
Julia: Nothing much. I'm really tired!
Just going to sleep now babe. And you?

😍

Jackson: I'm in the club standing behind
you..

2) Adam's Phone

Adam: Hi! I've found this phone.
You're the first in the contact list.
Could tell your friends it's been found?
Alex: Which friend?
Adam: The one whose name is at the top
of your screen
Alex: AHAHA oh yeah lol
Adam: So, can you tell him I've found it?
Alex: Hi It's Adam. Someone's found your
phone.

3) The movie

Lana: Have you seen the movie Bad Teacher?

Sophia: No

Lana: That's probably what we are gonna watch on Friday and it looks really funny

Sophia: Cool vaginas

Lana: Right........

Sophia: Beans? Stupid autocorrect!

Lana: LMFAO!!!!

4) Flogging!

Williamson: It was pretty tame yesterday But Saturday night could be flogger by Different

Tiffany: It's our day off together, I want to try to do something fun for her at least

Williamson: Ok

Tiffany: Flogger?? Lmao Auto correct is a trip

5) So, I was tight then?

Jeff: ...out on a wing and say you're either
a Banker
or financial analyst
David: That's an easy wing!
Jeff: haha, so I was tight then?
David: Nice correct fail again – hahaha
Jeff: Noo, that's it. Give me a minute.
I need to re-evaluate my life
David: Deep breath

6) make my bed...

Brad: Mom, why do I have to make the bed
everyday when I'm going to sleep in it
again?
Mom: Why do you wipe when you are
going to shit again?

7) Fingering the girl

Paul: **Okay, I'm just gonna go home and cry**
CEEC: No. Go finger the girl.
Oh god.
I mean find Fucking tablet
Paul: **hahaha**

8) Moist acne

Matt: **Can you trim my moist acne**
Lucy: **What**
Matt: **Oh my! Sorry.**
Moustache
Lucy: **Hahahaha**

9) Getting Drunk

Brooke: Plus, you are going to be my uber driver the entire time
I'm in town and I'm going to get drunk and sleep on my dad's body for a week.
Damian: WHAT? Did you proofread that last sentence there or are you into that sort of thing haha?
Brooke: Ommmmmg
I'm crying Boooaaattt
Damian: Hahaha

10) You are vehicular

Lovren: aww! Thank you ☺ Hahaha. Perfect indeed and I wish that was the case
Josh: You are vehicular!!
Beautiful*
Lovren: Hahaha. See your phone doesn't agree. Hahaha

11) Kobe You

Mallorney: Miss you
Alicey: I'm going to sleep..
Kobe you
Mallorney: I know
Alicey: Kobe!!!
Kobe You

Mallorney: Kobe 🏀
Alicey: Love you. Fuck!
Mallorney: Hahahaha

12) Getting ready and shower

Ryan: I'm going to check on the dog nod
and then I'm gonna cunt back
and shower and get ready
Lollipop: Lol! Eww. Haha.
Ok, baby.
Ryan: Hahaha Oops!

13) I try not

Mahberg: I try not to play with fire or poke beats

Snady: Pride... My face hurts

Mahberg: Bears

Snady: Lions???

Some people drop the beat, Dan pokes it.

Mahberg: It's called dub-skip

Snady: Dan – the white bread dubskip DVD and bluray

Mahberg: My initials are already DJ DJ bro. dubskip pioneer

14) All weekends

Jo: Sprints!

We will take it easy tomorrow and just work on form

Missie: No, we won't. Lol I rest all weekend, may as well milk myself tomorrow

Hahaha kill no milking

Jo: ahahah That was funny

Missie: Hahaha

15) You wanna go babdos?

Emy: I will be around for 6:15 xoxo
Josh: Ok. You wanna go to babdos?
Babdos? Babdos?
Emy: What?
Josh:Ducking nandos
Emy: Lol
Josh: Fucking nandos
Emy: Yes!!!! 😂 😂

16) To smoke or not to smoke

Catlyn: **To smoke or not to smoke that is the weed question**
To be or not to be, that is the real question
Millieu: **My dad's on this phone**
Catlyn: **...**

17) Gollum!

Arren: **I am not mom, I am golly**
You are precious; she is south bound
Jolly: **Southbound??**
Arren: **Holy typos/ auto correct, batman**
Jolly: **What did you mean??**
Arren: **I am Gollum. You are preciousssssssssssss**

18) You are so fatter

Rena: It has! You are so fatter Farr***
it is autocorrect You are beautiful I love
you
I love you. I am so sorry My phone hates
me
Excuse me while die internally
Ann: HAHAHAHAHA. I loveyou

19) Bringing a blanket

Alana: I will bring a blanket and we will
make it a cut dick date Hahahaha. OMG!
Dock**
Lemmy: Hahahaha
Alana: 😂

20) Open your pool

April: It is hot. It is supposed to get up to like 85 tomorrow

Lucy: I love it!!!

April: I think you should open your poop hole for me this weekend 😊

Lucy: WTF?

April: POOOOLL!!! I am laughing so hard

Lucy: I'm definitely not opening my poop hole for anyone!!!

21) You type good

Tyler: Hasn't really said anything since. Lol.

Vidan: XD yay

Tyler: He won't stop plowing me though. It is annoying. LMAO. Wait no. Following.

Vidan: You type good

Tyler: Shut up

Vidan: Lol

Tyler: It was auto-correct

Vidan: Mhm. Sure.

22) It's national coming out day

John: **Wait for me by the library fit the pep rally**
Savannah: **Ok, I will.**
John: **It's national coming out gay Day***
OMFG!
I think my phone knows... My Phone is onto us, Savannah!
The phone knows it all.

23) Coming Over

Paul: **U home?**
Edith: **Yea, watching the game**
Paul: **Good. I'm coming over,**
I'm bringing cold hermaphrodites with me
Edith: **Uh. No. Thanks bro**
Paul: **Hermaphrodites!! Heineken! Jesus crust.**
Christ!
Edith: **Lol. I'll unlock the door you freak**

24) Break her finger

Julian: **How did Emily break her finger?**
Lola: **Her finger got stuck in my butthole**
Julian: **WHAAATTT?!**
Lola: **Holyshit. My buckle. Belt buckle.**
Julian: **That is the funniest thing I have heard all day.**

25) Surprise dinner from Mother

Mom: **Are you hungry?**
Dave: **Starving**
Mom: **I thought you might be.
There is a huge surprise waiting for you in the kitchen. It's your favorite. Love Mom.**
Dave: **I hope it is your shaved pussy OMG!
Please don't read the last text. It was the worst autocorrect of my all life
I meant poooooorrrrrkkkkkk shaved pork.
I am so sorry, Ma.
Mom?**

26) Shits

Charlie: **Awwww. I miss you too**

Lovren: **don't think I'm weird but I am sleeping**

with that shit, you have left in the bathroom

Charlie: **WHAT?!?!**

Lovren: **Yea, it smells like you and it makes me feel better when you are not here.**

Charlie: **If you are trying to be cute or funny, it isn't working**

Lovren: **Ohhhhhh mmmmmyyyyy goooodddd**

******Shirts****

I am going to kill myself right now.

27) Red Breast!

Margaret: **I have an irkling**

Matthew: **Yeah! You know something strange though?**

In 8th grade, my best friend was a girl like you with red breasts

***RED HAIR!!**

28) New Room color

Jake: **Are you done painting Jason's living room yet?**
Josh: **yeah, just finished**
Jake: **What color is it again?**
Josh: **It is called period red**
Jake: **Dude. No. You are sick.**
Josh: **Holy shit. It is called Persian red!**
I got autocorrected.
Epic fail!
Jake: **ommmmgggggg. We are dying here.**

29) Finding a pencil for exam

Ore: **Hey.**
Can I get my pencil back?
I have an exam in 30.
Dave: **Yeah. I will get it out of my lover.**
Ore: **You and Dan are into some kinky stuff. Haha.**
Dave: ***Locker. Love it!**

30) A wrong Date!

So how was the date last night bro.
Did you score?
Finnidy: Not quite. First date we went to
have dinner and then
walked her home Then killed her in the
woods outside her house and left
Killing her seems a bit harsh.
Did she order the lobster and fillet mignon
at dinner or something?
Finnidy: ****KISSED** wtf!

31) I will be black

Missie: I will be black in a minute
Bose: Huh!!?
Missie: I meant BACK. Freaking auto correct.
I will be BACK. As far as I know,
I won't be black anytime soon.
Lolz.
Bose: 😂

32) Toby

Beth: Babe, I don't feel like cooking tonight.
Can you bring home human beef?
Toby: WTF Beth? I'm in a meeting.
Human beef? Are you high?
Beth: Hunan beef! The place that just opened on 7th avenue!
I'm laughing so hard I almost puked.
Toby: Jesus! I just laughed out loud and could possibly get fired now.
Order your human beef.
I will pick it up at 6. Love you.

33) Hamster Paradise

Taylor: I am a gangster.
I am a straight up G
the hamster life is life for me. STUPID
AUTO CORRECT!!!
Lola: Been spending most of their lives in
the hamster paradise
Taylor: Don't make fun of me...

34) Fun for Friday

Davidson: Can't wait to see you babe.
Hurry up and get here!
Pamela: Whoo hoo! It is Friday.
Screw the gym.
I'm getting pregnant tonight.
Davidson: Uh... Shouldn't we talk about
that first?
Pamela: HAHAHAHAHA oh my god!
I wrote pringles and
it autocorrected to pregnant
Davidson: I almost had a heart attack.

35) Worst Birthday Wish

Lily: **Happy birthday to you Happy birthday to you Happy birthday dead husband!**
Happy birthday to you.
Scott: **Thanks. I assume you meant "dear"**
Lily: **Ahhhhh Yes!! I mean that is a crazy autocorrect!**
Sorry babe.

36) Bad dialog

Thank you again for an amazing first date 😊

Chris: Anytime 😊 When is the 2nd date?

I can't wait to see those big beautiful nipples of yours

NO!

I am sorry.

I meant dimples.

My phone changed it I did not mean to write nipples

I am going to jump off a bridge right now...

37) A brief meeting

Dr. Joe: Hi Jan, are you coming to the meeting at 4?

Jane: I will be there

Dr. Joe: Great. Please meet me in my office at 3:30 so we can have a brief cunnilingus before hand

Jane: Excuse me?

Dr. Joe: I have no words. I typed conference and my phone changed it. I am so sorry.

Jane: Wow. It is fine 😂

38) Time with a client

Maddie: Sorry, I was with a clitoris

Fred: LMFAO

Maddie: OMG!!! I was with a client This Phone!

39) Cutting to the bone

Phillips: No worries
**Dami: I really need you to bone
with me in about 10 minutes OMG – I
meant come not bone.**
Hahaha
**Phillips: Lol! Best typo ever. Not sure
that's an appropriate Work time activity**

40) Stepping into my office,
Baby

**ICE: Or you can give my info In my office
Knock me up when you get a chance
LMAO... hit me up OMG**
Joe: I will be right over
**ICE: Lol
You are funny Stupid auto correct**

41) Bad Timing

Principal: How does sex sound for tomorrow?
Omg. Omg. Omg.
I meant six. six. six

42) Courtroom Drama

Sarah M: Can we set up a phone call for this afternoon?
Today is not good.
I will be in and out of cunt all day.
Tomorrow will be better
Auto correct. I meant court.
I am sincerely sorry...
Sarah M: Well, this is awkward.
I will be in touch tomorrow then.
Thank you.

43) Licking the box

Lola: Mike, can you lick my box?
Mike: OMG! I mean lock my cash box!
Damn auto correct
Lola: Sure it was ☺

44) Toilet time

Fred: OMG! I'm sorry am running late.
I have been stuck on the toilet for over an
hour!
Matt J: Oh TMI.
If you are that sick stay home Nancy
cover for you.
Feel better soon. Matt
Fred: What? TMI? I am not sick
Matt J: You just said you have been on the
toilet if
You are that sick just stay home.
Fred: SH*T! That was supposed to be
toilet
OMG! It did it again TOLLWAY. maybe I
should go home ☺

45) Animal Instincts

Paulina: **Sorry forgot to text you wairus that the deposits were made**

Boss Lady: **Are you calling me a wairus?**

Paulina: **Lol. OMG! Sorry that was supposed to be earlier NOT wairus**

Boss Lady: **I know I have put on some weight... anyway thanks!**

Paulina: **OMG!! I am dying right now!**

46) SNL takes over auto correct

Susan: **Hi Mr. Harrison, I need to take 6 days off work Next week for a family emergency Who would I speak to about that?**

Hi, please head down to the HR dept and speak with Jon DICKINABOX!

I apologize. I meant Jon Dickinson.

That was a SNL.

Skit my phone inserted to be a wise guy.

Susan: **I know what it is. Thanks.**

47) Dick Jokes

Maureen: **Did the issue with the Canadian order get resolved?**

Paul: **Not yet. It is still being worked on.**

Maureen: **Okay. Please make sure the dick gets ejaculated.**

Yikes. I mean, the dick gets escalated

The TICKET gets ESCALATE.

I am sorry.

Paul: **Got it. Will do.**

48) Dead Boss

Lindsey: Dead Boss, the solicitor said he
appreciated your offer,
but he was not sure about car agora D. He
said he would
like to have a meeting with you a nod you
should meet him
in the entrance ball.
Kind farts. Your secretary.
Boss: Lindsay, just to let you know that I
am not dead.
I do not know what you mean you mean by
car agora D,
we do not have an entrance ball, and farts
are not kind.
You are in big trouble!

49) Running Late

Steven: **Running a big behind**
Loveth: **What? As your supervisor I don't**
think it would be appropriate
to comment on your text.
But oh I want to.
Steven: **Haha it was supposed to be bit**
not big
Loveth: **And here is one for damn you auto**
correct.
Just so you know, I have been running a
big belly.
Don't criticize your behind.

50) The Job Interview

Mr. Jonathan: **Hello Ms. Sarah, this is Jonathan from KPMG.**
I just wanted to confirm your interview at 1:30 pm tomorrow
Ms. Sarah: **Hello Mr. Jonathan.**
Yes, I will be there.
Thank you for confirming.
I look forward to sleeping with you.
speaking

51) Mind if I Pump you later

Employee: **Very cool! Mind if I pump you later then?**
Jaime: **Um, excuse me?!**
Employee: **Oh god! I'm so sorry.**
I meant, is it cool if I pimp you later?
join (not pump or pimp) So embarrassing
Jaime: **And completely inappropriate, perhaps?**

52) Game of Throbs

Matty: Thinking of you
Joe: Was watching game of
throbs with mon ^^ GAME OF THROBS
A song of boners HAHAHAHA
Matty: Just fell off my bed.
You are amazing
Joe: Laughing so hard
Matty: Best auto correct yet *D

53) Ducking Phone

Mum: Hey son, I picked up the new dick
today.
It's so cute OMFG! I meant dick
DICK DICK!! I HATE THIS
DICKING PHONE DUCKING DICK HOW
THE DUCK
DO YOU TURN THIS DICKING THING OFF
Jason: Hahahahahaha.
Farting so hard.
I'm crying.

54) Gonna go get time

Lovren: **I'm gonna go get some penis and watch in treatment**
Penis Penis Holy Shit Pizza
I can't believe that just happened!
Brandon: **I'm saving that**
Lovren: **The devil really is in this phone**

55) Black Cherry

Joe: **Haha! Gross**
Lawley: **Fucking autocirrey**
Dude spinach is nasty nuts. It's in my racuolu.
It's food Ravioli
OMG! It was so easier to type on my fucking blackcherry Duck...
Joe: **That makes me lol.**

56) Retribution

Mensah: **Dad, do you have any idea where my diploma is?**

Dad: **It is in your mother's anus**

*anus

*anus

Mensah: **Uh...**

Dad: **In her anus Jesus Mary and Joseph upstairs in her house in storage**

Mensah: **Wow. Ok. I will search Mum's anus. Thanks dad**

57) Tulips

Mom: **Great news Grandma is homosexual!**

Lolly: **Okay?**

Mom: **Homo hot lips**

Hot tulips

I am getting fisted now Frustrated Grandma is home From hospital

Lolly: **Hahaha. Homo hot lips!?**

58) Death Vibrator

Husband: **Made it to six fags
with the dearth vibrator mask
*flags
Death vibrator Dearth vader
Farther vader Dearth Darth**

Wife: **Hahahahaha** 😂

59) Cumming

Amy: **My cunt is humming My cunt is
coming My AUNT is roaming MY AUNT IS
COMING
Ferret Grrr
GOD DAMSEL
I'm done**

60) Auto Cart Socks

Caitlin: **Did you feather pussy out who error you horse**
Marie: **What?!**
Caitlin: **Find orange who egregious your hole?**
Marie: **Wow! My auto carts socks tonight.**
Caitlin: WTF
Marie: **My auto corrects sick tonight**

61) Auto crustacean

DX: **Want me to come over?**
Jane: **No – my parents are homeless**
HOME
Stupid auto crustacean
I mean auburn cock rocket FUCK MY LIFE SAVER.
I'm JUST CALLING YOU
DX: **A simple "maybe later" would have sufficed!** 😂

62) Duck husks

Momma: Are you sore Do ducks have jackets Did muck save maggots Ughhhh Does husk make gaggles Never mind
Dave: What!
What... I just.. what..

63) A ring giving

Dad: Dan, can you give me a ring My penis is stuck
Stuck in the muck Stuck in the butt What the fuck
Dan: What!! Just Whatt!!

64) Megan to Chris

Megan: My Cock won't get out of my cat My cat won't get out of my cat Ruckus. I mean my cat won't get out of my cat Fuck. Bitch is in my car Butch! Jesus Taliban I HIV up

65) Jesus Chalupa

Jake: Ok. Good love you have Bar
Babe Jesus chalapu
NOW HOW DID THAT FUCKING HAKEEM?!
Happen. Not jaleel
Binta: LMAO
Jake: Hakeem
Jesus ...

66) Doodie

James: What up doodie
*doodie Fucj Fuckkkk
*Nagaland Seriously...
That's not even close DOODIE
DUDE

67) Elevator Call on Joey

Joey: So you obviously love me a little bit

Dan: Screw you Joey. Ding ding oh what
was that oh yes, the elevator
cause you're not on my level.
I won this fight.
Were over forreal this time

68) To the same person

Mark: She's pretty... don't think she's gf
material thought...
she told me she doesn't want kids and
hates sports?!?
Wtf?! Who HATES sports?

Britney: Awkward

Mark: Jesus H Christ
I am an asshole I'm sorry.

69) Feeling..

Jane: I'm feeling Ugly..

Paul: That makes you special ☺

Jane: ....

70) A bad Show

Is you good

Dan: No not really tbh, thing have been

hard lately ▪▪▪

Oh I meant the show..

71) Too Much Love

Lana: I don't want to be toxic no more

Mike: Okay I'll leave you alone

Lana: No I'll leave you alone

Mike: I'm own

Lana: ok

72) Supervisor's text

Dominique: **Is this Montana?**

Patrick: **No, This Patrick LMAO Yeah, it's me Who is?**

Dominique: **Dominique from Dr. Reddy's office**

Patrick: **Oh, I'm so sorry, yes, this Montana..**

73) Crazy Crazy Baby

Eddy: **Wyd baby girl**
Karen: **I'm at therapy wyd love**
Eddy: **Therapy for what?**
Karen: **Mental Health**
Eddy: **Oh.. you crazy crazy** 😂

74) Pizza vs Carrots

I was having a pizza tonight and though of you..
Lola: I had some baby carrots earlier and thought of your dick. Bye

75) Dead Diego

Luke: How do you think you did?
Diego: On what?
Luke: The final bro
Diego: It's tomorrow
Luke: It was today at 10:35...
!!!???
DIEGO?!?
Ehy?!?!

76) Not so Single

Patrick: U single?
Laura: Not really, I'm kinda talking to someone
Patrick: Damn what y'all talking about

77) LOL

Mum: Sam your a disappointment
Sam: You're*

78) Tip Forgetter

Waitress: Hey Boys, so glad you left me your numbers, I think you guys actually forgot something at the restaurant ;)
Guys: What did we forgot? ;) You? ☺ Sure hope it was!
Waitress: No the rest of my tip....

79) The Pack?

Jordan: **You got the Pack?**

Marika: **What does that mean Jordan you got the pack**
you confuse me with this language

Jordan: **Lol I'm sorry, wrong person**

Marika: **Ok I guess that's what it means wrong**
person thank you

80) Go Fuck Ass in the Car

Jane: **What did you decide about Minnesota?**

Thomas: **I'm not sure yet**

Jane: **Can you stop at Mimi's and get her debit car**
and go fuck ass in my car oh my God that is
totally not what I said,
I said go put gas on my car!

Thomas: **Yeah I can** ☺ ☺

Jane: **That's the worst talk to text AutoCorrect**
I have ever heard

81) A charging Vibrator

Client: Can I buy it about 3? That's the time I'm off work
Seller: Yeah
Client: Bet I'll text you when I'm on the way Charging the vibrator so we can take it and play hehe Omg wrong person my fucking fault!

82) Wire Fire

Mum: John what's the wire fire code?
John: What?!?
Mum: Wifi code... fucking autocorrect!

83) Ok...

Den: I don't understand why you're angry
with me
if you allowed me to go You said "OK,
Den"
Julia: If you're so silly and you can't see
the difference between "OK" and
"OK, Den", It's not my problem!
Den: ...

84) Ruined relationships

Helen: What's up?
**Mettew: I've just ruined a relationship that
lasted for 5 years**
Helen: Oh I'm sorry...
Mattew: It's fine. It wasn't mine!

85) 65$

Kate: Hi, will you lend me 65$ until
Friday?
Dany: Ok, will you give me your powder
and foundation?
Kate: Sure
Dany: Kate would write that's pointless
because nothing can save my face
So give my friend phone back!

86) Wine sucks but...

Kim: That wine you bought sucks!
Gary: It cost 45$!
Kim: Oh sure.. I can already feel the
subtle fruit flavor
of the Tuscan fields

87) Do not go

Ann: Sometimes people invite you and you don't go.
Then they'll do it again, and you don't go again.
And then they stop doing it.
Mark: I lost my job that way once...

88) New clothes

Emily: I bought some new clothes
afterwards I will
show them to you
Mike: I can't wait to take them off and throw you in bed tonight.
Emily: Alex we are in the family chat!!
Mike: ....

89) Writing you

Natalie: What are you doing?
Bart: I'm writing to the best girl in the world

Natalie: How lovely 😍
Bart: She isn't answering.That's why I'm writing to you

90) Wedding

Freddy: What kind of wedding do you want?
Jessie: With you!
Freddy: 😍😍😍
Jessie: You'll serve the dishes and set the tables

91) Where are you?

Kevin: Laura Where are you?

Laura: I'm home and you?

Kevin: I've been in the car for an hour

Laura: Oh, Kevin I'm sorry. I was dressing and I forgot...

I decided I was doing it to take a selfie

Btw, can you like it? 😁

92) Smoothie

Leo: What are you drinking?

Abigail: A smoothie, it's very healthy!

Leo: What's in there?

Abigail: Fruits, berries, vodka, and antidepressants

Leo: 😈

93) New girlfriend..

**Paul: My girlfriend and I broke up because
I liked 5 of
your photo on IG! This means you're my
girlfriend now!
Wanna go to the movies?
Ehiii?!?**

94) LOL

**Anne: Andrew, don't forget that my mother
is coming today!
Hope you took out the trash and washed
the dishes like I asked.
You're taking the kids today**

Tom: Thank God I'm Tom! 😁

95) On Face

**Philippe: You're cool and brave on the internet.
But would you look me in the face and repeat all of that?
Julius: OK, Send me your photo!**

96) you like it

**Sofy: I think I'm gonna dye my hair black.
Alan: Why?
Sofy: I'll pierce my nose and lips. and I'll get tattoo.
Alan: Why? don't do that!
Sofy: Why not? You like it!**

Liked by Alan

97) Big Problem

Todd: **I have a problem, man**

Drake: **Continue**

Todd: **Ok, listen**

Drake: **Well?**

Todd: **When close my eyes, I can't see anything**

Drake: 😅

98) Help Me

Debby: **Dad help me!**

I was kidnapped

They want me to marry him.

Dad: **What car did they put you in?**

Debby: **I think it was a Black BMW X5**

Dad: **Well, be happy!**

Mum and I are happy for you!

99) We meet?

Stan: **Hi Can we meet?**
Karen: **I have a boyfriend**
Stan: **You don't have any photo with him. You can just say that you don't want to meet.**
Karen: **OK, I just don't wanna meet a homeless person who lives on the streets**
Stan: **haha, why do you think so?**
Karen: **Because you don't have any photos with your house!**

100)   Pregnant

Katy: **I don't know if I told you... I'm pregnant!** 😍
Olivia: **Oh God.. what are you going to do?**
Katy: **What do you mean? I'm married. It's fine** 😁
Olivia: **Oh! Sorry, sometimes I forget we are already 30!** ☹️

101)   30 minutes

Unknown: **Mum wants you to call her**
Fred: **Who is this?**
Unknown: **Andrea**
Fred: **You got the wrong number.**
But thanks anyway! I called my mom,

and we had a 30-minute talk 😅

102)   Just married

Frank: **If I'm so bad then why are you**
dating me?
Dana: **Cause we're married**

103)   Beautiful and
Funny

Patrick: **No, you're not silly!**
you're smart and beautiful and funny ☺
Helena: **And not a single word about me**
being skinny..
Thank YOU!

104)   Playing..

Hailey: **Hi, What are you doing?**
Trevor: **Playing DOOM.**
Hailey: **Why do you need those monsters**
when
you have me?
Trevor: 😂

105)   Fat Butt

Chloe: **If I could see my fat butt I would**
stop eating donuts!
Fortunately,

My butt in behind me 😂

106)   Leave school

Son: Dad I decided to leave the school.
Dad: Okay then, but there's one thing you never forget son
Son: What is it?
Dad: You've got to smile while delivering pizza

107)   Blacklisted

Billy: Mum, why have you blacklisted my number?
Mum: I had to, because of all that spam
Billy: What Spam?!
Mum: Things like "Mom, put some money on my phone!",
"Mom, I need a new jacket!" and "Mom, I need some cash, pronto!"

108) Mum's Birthday

Paul: Dad can you give me 100$? It's for Mum's birthday present!
Dad: I'll give you 50$ It's not right that your present should be more expensive than mine! ☺

109) Adopted

Morgan: Mum tell me the truth: was I adopted?
Mum: Do you think that, given a choice, your dad and I would have picked someone like you?

110)   Old phone

Bob: **Dad, that old cell phone of yours that you gave me...**

Dad: **Yes?**

Bob: **Well I was rummaging through it, last night**

Dad: **And?**

Bob: **Mom sure looks cool in these photos**

Dad: **Oh, crap...**

111)   Do not touch Kevin!

Sharon: **Mum, my room is not a mess! In there everything is exactly where it needs to be**

Mum: **Really? What about that layer of dust on the table?**

Sharon: **I've got important phone numbers written on it**

Mum: **Is that so? And what about that spider in the corner?**

Sharon: **Don't touch Kevin! He's done nothing to you!**

112)   Girl party..

Dad: **Dude, you should be here with us!**
Come get a breath of fresh country air
Philippe: **No way**
Dad: **You don't know what are you missing!**
We have got beer and barbecues!
And girls are ready to party!
Philippe: **Dad, won't buy this a second time!**
You and Mum will have
to dig those potatoes without me!
Period

113)   Bit trouble

Dad: **Son, you're in a big trouble.**
Ruben: **Why?**
Dad: **Because you're texting during lesson**
Ruben: **Are you serius? It's you who started it!**

114)   My Baby

Mike: **Hey babeeee, I can't go out tonight, Family Stuff** 😞
Rita: **Oh it's fine. I hope everything gets better love**
Mike: **Thanks babe. I'll talk to you later. I love u**
Rita: **Love you too**

Mike: **Hey Jenny, I'll be there at 7** 😏
Rita: **Who's Jenny?!?**
Mike: **oh shit...**

115)   So WET

Mum: **I'M so WET!!!!**
Tina: **Mom WTF?**
Mum: **What do you mean honey?**
Tina: **You're so wet?!**
Mum: **Yes, haven't you looked outside its pouring**

CPSIA information can be obtained
at www.ICGtesting.com
Printed in the USA
BVHW062036040521
606420BV00010B/2474